ماذا يجب أن تعرف عن خالقك؟
لشيخ محمد بن صالح العثيمين

what you must Believe about your Creator

This booklet is a translation of 'Faith in Allah' from the book,
'Sharh Hadeeth Jibra'eel' by Shaikh ibn Saleh al-Uthaimeen

with additional quotes from
'Aqeedah at-Tawheed' and 'Mujmal Aqeedah as-Salaf'
by Shaikh Salih ibn Fawzan ibn Abdullah al-Fawzan

Translated and Compiled by Shawana A. Aziz

Contents

Foreword

Foreword adapted from the book,
'Aqeedah at-Tawheed'
by Shaikh Saleh ibn Fawzan ibn Abdullah al-Fawzan

'Al-Aqeedah (faith)' is what a person takes as a religion. It is said, 'He has a good Aqeedah' meaning, 'He is protected from doubts.'

Aqeedah is an action of the heart - which is to believe and affirm something in the heart.

In the Sharee'ah, Aqeedah is the belief/faith in Allah, His Angels, His Books, His Messengers, the Last Day and Predestination - its good and evil. These are called the Pillars of Eeman (faith).

The Sharee'ah is divided into two parts; Beliefs and Actions.

(a) Beliefs are issues that are not related to how an act is performed such as belief in the Lordship of Allah, the obligation to worship Allah (alone) and belief in the other afore-mentioned pillars of Eeman (faith). These are called Asliyah - the basic foundation.

(b) The latter part consists of issues related to how actions are performed like Salaat (prayer), Zakaat (charity), Sawm (fasting) and other rulings with regards to actions. These are termed as Far'eyyah - the branches, because their soundness or corruption is based upon the beliefs.

The c orrect Aqeedah is thus the foundation upon which the religion is based. It is the correct Aqeedah with which the actions are set aright as the Most High said, "So, whoever hopes for the meeting with his Lord, let him work righteousness and associate none as a partner in the worship of his Lord." [Soorah al-Kahf (18): 1 10]

"Indeed, it has been revealed to you (O Muhammad ﷺ) as it was to those (Prophets) before you, 'If you join others in worship with Allah, (then) surely (all) your deeds will be in vain, and you will certainly be among the losers." [Soorah az-Zumar (39): 65]

"So, worship Allah (alone) by performing religious deeds sincerely for His sake. Surely, the religion is for Allah only." [Soorah Zumar (39): 2]

These verses and numerous other narrations that have been related in this regard confirm that <u>actions are not accepted unless they are free from Shirk</u> (polytheism/associating partners with Allah).

It was therefore the main concern of the Messengers ﷺ to rectify the beliefs first. Sole worship of Allah and abandonment of worship to anything other than Him was their primary call as the Most High says, "Verily, We have sent among every Ummah (community, nation) a Messenger (proclaiming), 'Worship Allah (Alone), and avoid the Taghoot (everything that is worshiped other than Allah)." [Soorah An-Nahl (16): 36]

The first issue addressed by every Prophet was, "Worship Allah! You have no other Ilah (deity worthy of being worshiped) but Him." [Soorah al-A'raf (7): 59, 65, 73, 85]

It was said by Nuh , Hood , Saleh عليه السلام, Suhaib عليه السلام and all the other Prophets عليهم السلام to their nations. After being bestowed with Prophethood, the Messenger of Allah stayed in Mecca for thirteen years calling people to Tawheed and rectifying their Aqeedah because Aqeedah is the foundation upon which the entire structure of the Deen stands.

The Duaat (callers to the religion of Allah) and those who seek to guide others during every age followed the example of the Messengers and the Prophets who initiated their call with Tawheed (Oneness of Allah's worship) and correction of Aqeedah, and subsequently focusing upon the remaining commandments of the Deen (religion).

The Sources of Aqeedah and
the Manhaj (way) of the Salaf
in deriving and learning it

Aqeedah is Tawqeefiyah (which means that) beliefs cannot be established except with a proof from the Sharee'ah (religious texts) - there is no room for opinion and speculation.

The sources of Aqeedah are therefore restricted to what is mentioned in the Book and the Sunnah (Ahadeeth of the Prophet) because no one is more knowledgeable than Allah about the obligations due to Him and what He is free from - and after Allah - no one knows more about Allah other than His Messenger   .

The Manhaj (way) of the Salaf as-Saleh (the pious predecessors) and those who followed them was therefore restricted to the Book and the Sunnah. They believed, affirmed and implemented everything that was established in the Book and the Sunnah concerning the Rights of Allah. They disowned and rejected everything that was not established in either of these two sources.

Thus, no differences were found amongst them with regards to beliefs. Their belief was one and their Jama'ah was one because Allah supports whoever holds on to His Book and the Sunnah of His Messenger   with a unified position, correct Aqeedah and unity of Manhaj.

"Hold fast, all of you together, to the Rope of Allah (i.e. this Qur'an) and be not divided among yourselves." [Soorah aal-Imran (3): 103] and, "Then if there comes to you guidance from Me, then whoever follows My Guidance shall neither go astray nor fall into distress and misery." [Soorah Taha (20): 123]

They are therefore called 'the saved sect' for whom the Messenger testified safety (from the Hell-Fire) when he informed about the splitting of the Ummah (nation) into seventy-three sects - all of them in the Fire except one. When he   was asked about this one (saved sect), he   replied, "...that which I and my companions are upon this day." [narrated by Imam Ahmad]

The prophecy of Allah's Messenger   has come to pass. Some people have built their Aqeedah upon other than the Book and the Sunnah - such as Ilmul-Kalam - (argumentation based upon) the fundamentals of logic inherited from Greek philosophy. (thus) there occurred deviation from (the correct) Aqeedah, which further resulted in differing of the word, splitting of the Jama'ah and demolition of the united structure of Islam.

Causes of Deviation

Deviation from the correct Aqeedah is destruction and failure because the correct Aqeedah is the strong motivating force towards beneficial actions.

An individual without the correct Aqeedah can become a victim of misunderstandings and doubts that besiege him and make obscure (for him) the path to a blissful life - until his life narrows down upon him and he tries to break through this confinement by committing suicide. This has occurred to many people who have lost the guidance of the correct Aqeedah.

A society which is not governed by the correct Aqeedah is an animalistic society that has lost all components of a blissful life. Even if (such a) society possesses various elements of material life, it gradually leads to destruction - as is witnessed in the disbelieving communities.

It is such because (even) these material elements require direction and guidance in order to benefit from their qualities and advantages - and nothing can guide it except the correct Aqeedah. It is therefore necessary that the strength of Aqeedah should not be separated from the materialistic strength.

If you separate yourself from the correct Aqeedah by deviating to the false beliefs - then the materialistic strength becomes a means of destruction and degradation as is seen today in the disbelieving countries that own the materialistic (strength) but do not posses the sound Aqeedah.

Deviation from the correct Aqeedah has many causes, from the most important of them are:

1. Ignorance of the correct Aqeedah due

to turning away from learning and teaching it or lack of concern for it - until there arises a generation who is ignorant of the correct Aqeedah and that which contradicts it. The truth is then deemed to be falsehood and falsehood to be the truth - as Umar Ibn Khattab ؓ said, "Verily, the bonds of Islam will be destroyed one by one, when there arise in Islam people who do not know or recognize Jahiliyah (ignorance)."

2. Bigotry (ta'assub) towards the beliefs of

the ancestors - adhering to them even if they are false and forsaking everything that opposes them even if it is the truth.

Allah says, "When it is said to them, 'Follow what Allah has sent down.' They say, 'Nay! We shall follow what we found our fathers following.' (Would they do that!) Even though their fathers did not understand anything nor were they guided?' [Soorah al-Baqarah (2): 170]

3. Blind-Following (Taqleed) by accepting

people's statements concerning Aqeedah without knowing the proof or level of authenticity - as is the case of the Jahmiyyah, Mu'tazilah, Ash'aris, Soofis and others whereby they (blindly) followed their deviant scholars who preceded them and thus, they were misguided and went astray from the correct beliefs.

4. Extremism or Exaggeration (in honoring)

the Awliya (saints) and the Saliheen (righteous) through the following acts

Raising the Awliya and the Saliheen above their due status where it is believed that they bring benefits and prevent harm in a manner which none has the ability to do except Allah.

Taking the Awliya and the Saliheen as intermediaries between Allah and the creation in fulfilling needs and answering the duaa - until the matter turns into worshiping other than Allah.

Seeking nearness to their tombs through sacrifices, vows (nadhr), supplication, seeking aid and asking for help like what occurred among the people of Nuh   regarding the pious. They said, "You shall not leave your gods, nor shall you leave Wadd, Suwa, Yaghuth, Ya'uq nor Nasr (names of the idols)." [Soorah Nuh (71):23]

Such is also the case of the grave-worshippers of today in many countries.

5. Negligence in pondering over the universal and

Qur'aanic Ayaat (proofs, evidences, verses, lessons, signs, revelations, etc.) of Allah while being overwhelmed by the facts and figures of the material civilization - until people think that this is from man's ability alone. They glorify man and attribute these accomplishments to man's endeavors and experiments alone - as Qaroon said, "This has been given to me only because of knowledge I possess." [Soorah al-Qasas (28): 78] and as man says, "This is for me (due to my merit)." [Soorah Fussilat (41): 50] "Only because of knowledge (that I possess) I obtained it." [Soorah az-Zumar (39): 49]

They do not ponder or look at the glory of the One, Who originated this universe and bestowed in it these magnificent wonders. He Who originated man and conferred upon him the ability to derive and utilize these benefits. "Allah has created you and what you make!" [Soorah as-Saffat (37): 96] "Do they not look in the dominion of the heavens and the earth and all things that Allah has created." [Soorah al-A'raf (7): 185]

"Allah is He, Who has created the heavens and the earth and He sends down water (rain) from the sky and thereby brought forth fruits as provision for you. He has made the ships to be of service to you – so that they may sail through the sea by His Command.

He has made rivers (also) to be of service to you. He has made the sun and the moon - both constantly pursuing their courses - to be of service to you. He has made the night and the day to be of service to you. He gave you of all that you asked for and if you count the Blessings of Allah, never will you be able to count them." [Soorah Ibraheem (14): 32-34]

6. Houses have become empty of the correct guidelines.

The Messenger of Allah   said, "Every child is born upon Fitrah (natural inborn instinct which recognizes Allah) but his parents make him a Jew, a Christian or a fire-worshiper." [Agreed upon] Parents thus play a big role in setting right the child's way of life.

7. Lack of importance for the means of teaching

and spreading (Islamic) knowledge in most of the Islamic world. More often, the methods of teaching do not give much importance to the religious part or they are careless in this regard from the start.

The means of transmitting knowledge whether textual, audio-visual or verbal have mostly become tools of destruction and misguidance or they are more involved in material and entertaining obsessions. People do not care about building (good) character, instilling the correct Aqeedah or combating misguided trends until there arises a generation who is defenseless against misguidance.

Means of Avoiding Deviation

1. Returning to the Book of Allah and the Sunnah of His Messenger to derive the correct Aqeedah just like as-Salaf as-Saleh. "The later part of this Ummah will not be corrected except by that which corrected its earliest part."

With this (it is also necessary to be) aware of the beliefs of the deviant groups. To know their doubts in order to refute them and warn against them - because he who does not know evil, tends to fall into it.

2. Giving importance to teaching the correct Aqeedah - the Aqeedah of as-Salaf as-Saleh - in different educational levels and giving it ample share of the syllabus and arranging precise examinations on the subject.

3. Organizing study of the pure books of the Salaf and staying far from books of deviant groups like the Sufis, the innovators, the Jahmiyyah, the Mu'tazilah, the Ash'aris, the Maturidis and others - except for knowing (their deviation) so as to refute what is in them of falsehood and warn against them.

4. Establishing Duat (callers) who revive the Aqeedah of the Salaf for the people and refute the misguidance of the deviated groups."

End of Foreword from 'Aqeedah at-Tawheed'

What you must believe about your Creator

"Eeman (belief/faith) in Allah comprises of four issues:

1. Eeman in the Existence of Allah

2. Eeman in the Rububiyah (Lordship) of Allah

3. Eeman in the Uluhiyyah (Worship) of Allah

4. Eeman in al-Asma was-Sifat

(the Names and Attributes) of Allah

Faith in Allah's Existence

Eeman in the Existence of Allah is to believe that Allah exists.

The Existence of Allah can be proven by (four ways):

1. Intellect
2. Senses and experiences
3. Fitrah (natural human instinct)
4. (Divine) Religions

1. Intellectual Proof
for the Existence of Allah

This universe runs in perfect order which cannot be interrupted. Its parts do not clash or collide into one another. "It is not for the sun to overtake the moon, nor does the night outstrip the day. They all float, each in an orbit." [Soorah Ya-Sin (36): 40]

Is it logical that this enormous universe with its perfect order could be the creator of itself?

No, it is not. This universe cannot be the creator of itself because this would mean that nothingness brought the creation into existence whereas nothingness cannot originate. So, it is impossible that this universe could be the creator of itself.

It is also not possible that this great universe could be a result of coincidence because it is running in a steady and marvelous order. Whenever there is a coincidence, it is more likely that it will not cause order. It is not possible that there occurs a coincidence except that it brings interruption.

Abu Hanifa (rahimahullah) was known for his intelligence and so there came to him a group of atheists asking him to prove the Existence of Allah.

Imam Abu Hanifa said, "Let me think," then he remarked, "I am thinking about a loaded ship that was tied to a port. The cargo unloaded itself without porters and the ship sailed away without a captain."

(Upon hearing this,) the atheists declared, "How can you say something like this! This is impossible. We cannot believe in it."

Imam Abu Hanifa (rahimahullah) replied, "If you do not believe in this then how do you believe in the sun, the moon, the stars, the sky and the earth – how can you believe that all these came into existence without an Originator?"

Allah points out this intellectual proof in His Saying, "Were they created by nothing or were they themselves the creators?" [Soorah at-Tur (52): 35]

A Bedouin was asked, "How do you know your Lord?"

The Bedouin could only reply with (the example of) that which was before him, so he said, "Droppings tell of a camel. Foot-prints tell of a traveler. The sky, the earth with mountain passes, seas with waves - do they not tell of the All-Hearer, the All-Seer?"

- Yes (they do), without doubt.

Shaikh Saleh ibn Fawzan al-Fawzan writes in Aqeedah at-Tawheed,

"It is necessarily known that every effect has a cause.

It is instinctively known even to a young child that if he is hit then there surely exists someone (or something) which caused it. So although he may have not seen the doer, he will ask, 'Who hit me?'

If he is told, 'Nobody hit you,' – it will not be acceptable to his mind that the hitting occurred without a doer...

This is why Allah says, 'Were they created by nothing, or were they themselves the creators?' [Soorah Toor (52): 35]

This verse mentions limited possibilities. Moreover, Allah mentions them in a negative form in order to assert that (the answer to) this is known by necessity and cannot be denied. He says, "Were they created by nothing?" meaning without a Creator? or did they create themselves? Verily, both these matters are false.

It is thus established that there exists a Creator Who Created them and He is Allah - there is no creator other than Him. Allah says, "This is the creation of Allah. So, show Me that which those (whom you worship) besides Him have created." [Soorah Luqman (31): 11] "Verily! Those whom you call upon besides Allah, cannot create (even) a fly, even if they combine together for the purpose." [Soorah al-Hajj (22): 73]

Although this challenge has been repeatedly brought up, no one has ever claimed to create anything. So, it is established that Allah is the Sole Creator, Who has no partners."

[end quote from Aqeedah at-Tawheed]

2. Senses and experiences
prove the Existence of Allah

We sense (the Existence of Allah) through the acceptance of our supplications. For example a man calls upon Allah saying, "O Allah." and Allah responds to his call, dispels his harm and grants his desires. This is because the man says, "O Allah." So there is a Lord Who Heard his call and Responded.

We Muslims read in the Qur'an that Allah responded to the supplications of His Prophets, "(remember) Nuh, when he cried (to Us) aforetime. We heard his invocation and saved him and his family from great distress " [Soorah al-Anbiya (21): 76]

"(Remember) Ayub, when he cried to his Lord, "Verily, distress has seized me, and You are the Most Merciful of all those who show mercy. So We answered his call. We removed the distress that was on him. We restored his family to him and the like thereof along with them as a mercy from Ourselves and a Reminder for all who worship Us." [Soorah al-Anbiya (21): 83-84]

Numerous verses can be found in this regard. (Real life) observations (too) testify to the Existence of Allah.

3. The Fitrah (natural human instinct) proves the Existence of Allah

When faced with calamities, man instinctively says, "O Allah." We are told that when an unexpected harm befalls, even some disbelievers and atheists - due to slip of the tongue and without realizing – say, "O Allah."

This occurs because the Fitrah of man testifies to the Existence of Allah, "(Remember) when your Lord brought forth from the Children of Adam, from their loins, their seed and made them testify as to themselves (saying), "Am I not your Lord?" They said, "Yes! We testify." [Soorah al-A'raf (7): 172]

Shaikh Fawzan writes in Aqeedah at-Tawheed,

"Firawn - who is famous for his pretense of denying the (existence of) Lord, was convinced about it inwardly, as Moosa said to him, "Verily you know that these signs have been sent down by none but the Lord of the heavens and the earth as clear (evidences)." [Soorah al-Isra (17): 102]

Allah said about Fir'awn and his people, "they belied them (those Ayaat) wrongfully and arrogantly, though their own selves were convinced thereof." [Soorah An-Naml (27): 14]

Similarly, today the denial of the atheist is also superficial and out of stubbornness. Otherwise, they surely affirm within themselves that there is nothing that exists except that it has an originator. There is no creation except that it has a creator. There is no trace except that it has someone who formed that trace. He, the Exalted, says, "Were they created by nothing, or were they themselves the creators? Or did they create the heavens and the earth? Nay, but they have no firm belief." [Soorah at-Toor (52): 35-36]

Consider all parts of this world, you will find it testifying to the existence of its Originator, Creator and Owner.

Denial and rejection of a Creator is like denying and rejecting knowledge - No difference. (Because the correct knowledge proves the existence of the Creator).

The atheist who boast about their denial of the Lord's existence, do so out of pride and lack of sound intellect and ideologies. He who is like them has revoked his intelligence and invited people to scoff at him. As the poet says,

"How can Allah be disobeyed and rejected by the jahid (the denier), (while) in everything, there is a sign which points out that he is waahid (One)."

[end quote from Aqeedah at-Tawheed]

4. (Divine) Religions
prove the Existence of Allah

If man was to consider all the religions, he will realize that the One, Who revealed and legislated these religions, is the Lord.

Allah says, "Do they not then consider the Qur'an carefully? Had it been from other than Allah they would surely have found therein much contradictions." [Soorah an-Nisa (4): 82]

Consistency and compatibility of the Qur'an, lack of contradictions (in the Qur'an), Qur'anic verses confirming each other – all this proves that the Qur'an was revealed from Allah.

The fact that this religion - rather all the Divine religions' being in complete conformity to the well-being of the slaves is a proof that they are from Allah. However, all the religions have been distorted and changed by those who oppose it, "there are some who displace words from (their) right places." [Soorah an-Nisa (4): 46] But all the religions that were revealed upon the Prophets testified to the Existence of Allah, His Wisdom and Knowledge.

Faith in the Oneness of Allah's Lordship

Rabb (Lord) means

    (i) the Creator

    (ii) the Owner

    (iii) the One in Control of all affairs

This is the meaning of Allah's Lordship (i.e., Allah is the Sole Creator, Owner and the One, in Control of all affairs). None of these benefit (or complete one's Faith in Allah's Lordship) without the other.

Allah is the Creator, Who originated everything from non-existence.

"The Originator of the heavens and the earth."
[Soorah al-Baqarah (2): 117]

"All the praises and thanks be to Allah,
the (Only) Originator of the heavens and the earth."
[Soorah Fatir (35): 1]

So He Who originated the universe from nothingness is the Creator. He is the Owner of what He created and He is Alone in his Ownership just like He is Alone in its Creation. Ponder over the Saying of Allah in Soorah al-Fatihah,

مالك يوم الدين

"Maalik of the Day of Recompense."
and in the sab'eeyah dialect,

ملك يوم الدين

"Malik of the Day of Recompense."

A remarkable meaning is identified when both Maalik and Malik are taken into consideration. Al-Maalik is more comprehensive than al-Malik with regards to control but al-Malik may sometimes not include the action of controlling and therefore one could be al-Malik but not al-Maalik. Allah is described with both al-Malik and al-Maalik – and thus the meaning becomes more profound with regards to Allah.

We thus say that Allah is Alone in His Dominion like He is Alone in His (Act of) Creation. Similarly, He is Alone in controlling all the affairs - even the disbelievers affirmed this. If they are asked who runs the affairs of the universe, they will say, 'Allah Alone runs the affairs.'

Shaikh Salih al-Fawzan writes in Mujmal Aqeedah as-Salaf,

"...even Iblees, who is the head of Kufr said, "O my Lord! Because you misled me..." [Soorah al-Hijr (15): 39] and "By Your Might, then I will surely mislead them all." [Soorah as-Saad (38): 82] So he confessed the Lordship of Allah and took an oath by His Might. Similarly, all the disbelievers confessed the Lordship of Allah like Abu Jahl, Abu Lahab and other heads of Kufr.

Allah says, "If you ask them who created them, they will surely say, "Allah" [Soorah Zukhruf (43): 87] "Say, 'In Whose Hands is the sovereignty of everything (i.e. treasures of each and everything)? He protects (all) while against Whom there is no protector, if you know." They will say, "(All that belongs) to Allah." [Soorah al-Mu'minoon (23): 88-89]

"Say, "Who provides for you from the sky and from the earth? Or who owns hearing and sight? Who brings out the living from the dead and brings out the dead from the living? Who disposes the affairs?" They will say, "Allah." Say, "Will you not then be afraid of Allah's punishment (for setting up rivals in worship with Allah)?" So they confessed all this.

During times of hardship they would solely invoke Allah because they knew that Allah Alone can take them out of hardships, and their false god and idols did not posses the power to rescue them from deadly situations. Allah says, "When harm touches you upon the sea, those that you call upon besides Him vanish from you except Him (Allah Alone). But when He brings you safely to land, you turn away (from Him). Man is ever ungrateful." [Soorah al-Isra (17): 67]

He, who believes <u>only</u> in this category of Tawheed (i.e., Rububiyah) does not enter Islam and will not be saved from the Fire. The disbelievers for instance confessed the Oneness of Allah's Lordship but their acceptance did not enter them into Islam. Allah called them disbelievers (Mushrikeen) and ruled that they will burn in Fire forever despite their belief in the Lordship of Allah.

With this becomes manifest the mistake of those writers who follow the way of the philosophers – when they explain Tawheed to mean affirming the Existence of Allah and affirming that Allah is the Sustainer, etc.

We say to them that this is not the Aqeedah with which Allah sent the Messengers. The Kuffar, the Mushrikeen and even Iblees affirmed the Lordship of Allah. Everybody affirms and confesses this category of Tawheed. The Messengers were not sent to ask people to affirm that Allah is the Creator, the Sustainer, the One Who gives life and causes death because this is not enough and does not save one from the punishment." [end quote from Mujmal]

The Message of all the Messengers was establishment of Tawheed al-Uluhiyyah as has been mentioned before and will be further exaplained, see. pg. 35

"He (Allah) arranges (every) affair
from the heavens to the earth."
[Soorah as-Sajdah (32): 5]

A Bedouin was asked, "By what do you know your Lord?" He replied, "Through revoking of one's intentions and dismissing one's interest."

Sometimes, man firmly resolves to do something but a moment later he finds himself revoking his intentions. Perhaps something interests man and he works towards it but then he dismisses it without a reason. This proves that there is someone over you who governs the affairs – and He is Allah.

Question: How do you say that Allah is Alone in His creation whereas Allah Himself affirms (the attribute of) creation for His creatures. He has called His creatures as, 'creators.' (in the Qur'an) and in a Hadeeth of Prophet it will be said to the artist (on the Day of Resurrection), "Bring to life that which you created."

Reply: The creation of man is not creation in reality because creation means originating (bringing into existence) from non-existence. When man creates something he does not originate it from non-existence. He only manipulates a thing from one shape to another.

Similarly, if it is asked (with regards to the Attribute of) al-Malik (the Owner), "How do you say that Allah is Alone in His Ownership whereas Allah affirmed ownership for others besides Him. He says in the Qur'an, "Except from their wives or that which their right hands own..." [Soorah al-Muminoon (23): 6] and He said, "or whereof you own the keys." [Soorah an-Nur (24): 61]

Reply: Ownership of man is not like the Ownership of Allah because the Ownership of Allah includes everything and is Absolute without restrictions whereas the ownership of man does not include everything and is restricted.

For example, a watch which is with me is not owned by you and the watch that is with you is not owned by me. So, it is a restricted ownership.

Similarly, the creation's ownership is not an absolute ownership because I cannot do anything I desire with the watch. I am restricted by the Sharee'ah (legislations of Islam) which is the authority. So if one wants to break his watch then this is not permissible for him because the Messenger prohibited wastage of money. So how about damaging it? Therefore, the scholars say that a man, even if a sane adult, who has wife and children, is a spendthrift and does not spend with responsibility, (then) he should be restricted from (spending) his wealth.

Allah, on the other hand, does with His Dominion as He Wills. He gives life and causes death. He causes sickness and He cures. He blesses His creation with richness and He afflicts them with poverty. We believe that Allah does what He Wills along with the belief that He does not do anything except for Wisdom.

There is thus a difference between the Ownership of the Creator and the ownership of the creation. We thus know that our statement, "Allah is alone in His Dominion" is correct and nothing is excluded from it (i.e., Allah's Dominion).

Similarly, running the affairs of the universe could be for man with regards to handling his servants or those under his patronage or his car, etc., but this running of affairs is not like Allah's running the affairs.

Running of affairs by man is deficient and restricted. Deficient because man does not posses control over it in the absolute sense. Perhaps, man owns a camel but the camel disobeys him. Perhaps, man controls his son but the son opposes him. It is thus restricted control and moreover, man can only control those things which Allah has given him power over. With this proves true our saying, "Allah Alone controls the affairs of the universe," just like the saying, "Allah is Alone in His Creation and Dominion."

Shaikh Saleh ibn Fawzan al-Fawzan
writes in Aqeedah at-Tawheed,

Tawheed ar-Rububiyah necessitates Tawheed al-Uluhiyah

Tawheed ar-Rububiyah necessitates Tawheed al-Uluhiyah i.e., he who declares Tawheed ar-Rububiyah and affirms that there is no Creator, Provider or Controller of the Universe except Allah - then he is required to proclaim Tawheed al-Uluhiyah – i.e., no one deserves any form of worship except Allah, none is to be invoked and sought help from except Allah, none is to be relied upon except Allah, none is to be offered sacrifices and avowed to except Allah and no worship is performed except for Allah alone.

Tawheed ar-Rububiyah is a proof of Tawheed al-Uluhiyah and thus Allah has primarily used Tawheed ar-Rububiyah as a proof against the deniers of Tawheed. He says, "O mankind! Worship your Lord (Allah) Who created you and those who were before you so that you may become pious. Who has made the earth a resting place for you and the sky as a canopy and sent down water (rain) from the sky and brought forth therewith fruits as a provision for you. Then do not set up rivals unto Allah (in worship) while you know (that He Alone has the right to be worshiped)." [Soorah al-Baqarah (3):21-22]

Allah thus ordered them with Tawheed al-Uluhiyah - which is His worship - and He presented as a proof - Tawheed ar-Rububiyah which is that Allah created the people of the earlier times and the latter generations. He created the sky and the earth and all that is between them; the blowing of the wind, sending down of the rain, the growing of the plants, the production of fruits which is the provision of the slaves. So it is not befitting for man to associate partners with Allah - such partners, whom he knows that they have not done any of the above or anything else besides that.

It is a natural instinct to affirm Tawheed al-Uluhiyah which is proved by Tawheed ar-Rububiyah because every person clings to the origin of his creation and the source of his benefit and harm. He then turns to the means which bring him closer to Him, please Him and strengthen the bond between them. Thus, Tawheed ar-Rububiyah is a door to Tawheed al-Uluhiyah and thus Allah used it as a proof against the Mushrikeen (those who associate a partner with Allah), Allah says in the Qur'an

"Say, 'Whose is the earth and whosoever is therein? If you know!' They will say, 'It is Allah's!' Say, 'Will you not then remember?'

Say, 'Who is (the) Lord of the seven heavens, and (the) Lord of the Great Throne?' They will say, 'Allah.' Say, 'Will you not then fear Allah.'

Say, 'In Whose Hand is the sovereignty of everything (i.e. treasures of each and everything)? And He protects (all), while against Whom there is no protector, if you know.' They will say, '(All that belongs) to Allah.' Say, 'How then are you deceived and turn away from the truth?" [Soorah al-Mu'minoon (23): 84]

"Such is Allah, your Lord! None deserves worship but He, the Creator of all things. So worship Him (Alone)." [Soorah al-An'aam (6): 102]

So, Allah used His Oneness in Lordship as a proof to establish that He alone deserves to be worshiped.

The slave cannot be a Muwahhid (one who believes in Tawheed in the correct manner) by affirming Tawheed ar-Rububiyah alone - until he declares Tawheed al-Uluhiyah and establishes it. The Mushrikeen used to proclaim Allah's Oneness in Rububiyah but it did not qualify them to enter Islam. The Messenger of Allah fought them while they were declaring that Allah is the Creator and Provider, the One, Who gives life and death as Allah says, "If you ask them who created them, they will surely say, 'Allah.'"[Soorah Zukhruf (43): 87]

"Indeed if you ask them, 'Who has created the heavens and the earth?' They will surely say, 'The All-Mighty, the All-Knower created them." [Soorah az-Zukhruf (43): 9]

"Say, 'Who provides for you from the sky and from the earth? Or who owns hearing and sight? And who brings out the living from the dead and brings out the dead from the living? And who disposes the affairs?' They will say, 'Allah.'" [Soorah Yunus (10): 31]

Plentiful similar verses can be found in the Qur'an. He, who claims that Tawheed is to affirm the Existence of Allah or declare that Allah is the Creator and the One, Who disposes the affairs of the Universe, and restricts himself to this definition - then he does not know the reality of Tawheed to which the Messenger called. Because he has halted at the affair, which necessitates (i.e., Tawheed ar-Rubibiyah) and he has abandoned what it necessitates (i.e., Tawheed al-Uluhiyah) or he has stopped at the proof and abandoned what it proves." [end quote from Aqeedah at-Tawheed]

- 33 -

Faith in the Oneness of Allah's Worship

Allah is the true ilah (the one who deserves to be worshiped). No one shares with Him this Right (of being worshiped) neither an Angel nor any Prophet. Therefore the call of all the Prophets from the first of them to the last of them was, "La ilaha illa Allah. (there is no ilah except Allah.)"

"We did not send any Messenger before you (O Muhammad   ) but We inspired him (saying), 'La ilaha illa Ana' (there is no ilah except Me), so worship Me (Alone)." [Soorah al-Anbiya (21): 25] "Verily, We have sent among every nation, a Messenger (proclaiming), "Worship Allah (Alone), and avoid Taghoot (false deities)." [Soorah an-Nahl (16): 36]

<u>So if someone believes in the Existence of Allah and believes in the Rububiyah of Allah but he worships others alongside Allah then he is not a believer in Allah until he singles out Allah in His Uluhiyyah.</u>

One might say that Allah approved the characteristic of Uluhiyyah (worship) for others besides Him. Allah said about Ibraheem, "Is it aliha (pl. of ilah) other than Allah that you seek?" [(37): 86] and Allah says, "Invoke not any other ilah along with Allah." [(28): 88] and other verses. So how can it be correct to say, "Allah is Alone in Uluhiyyah."

Reply: Uluhiyyah (worship) that is established for other than Allah is false Uluhiyyah. It is therefore absolutely denied, like in the saying of the Prophets to their nations, "Indeed, We sent Nuh to his people and he said, 'O my people! Worship Allah! You have no other Ilah but Him.'" [al-A'raf (7): 59] Those (other than Allah) are false ilah, "That is because Allah, He is the Truth and what they (the polytheist) invoke besides Him, it is Batil (false)." [al-Hajj (22): 62]

Shaikh Saleh al-Fawzan writes in Mujmal Aqeedah as-Salaf,

"Tawheed al-Uluhiyyah has (always) been the dispute between the Messengers and their nations. Every Messenger was sent summoning his nation, 'O my nation, worship Allah, there is no deity worthy of being worshiped except Him.' The Messengers did not summon their nations saying, 'O my people, verily Allah is your Lord' because all the nations believed in the Lordship of Allah.

The Messengers called their nation to worship their Lord alone for whom they affirmed Lordship and confessed that He is the Sole Creator, the Sole Sustainer and the One who runs the affairs of the universe. The Messengers called their nations to single out Allah just like they single out Him in Creation and the running of affairs. So the Messengers argued with their people based upon what they already affirmed.

The Qur'an mentions Tawheed ar-Rububiyah as an argument against the disbelievers and invites them to adhere to the necessary requirement of their belief. Oh disbelievers, if you accept that Allah is the Sole Creator, the Sole Provider and He Alone saves you from harm and destruction – then why do you turn towards others besides Him, those who have no authority in anything - neither creation, provision nor running the affairs of the universe, "Is then He, Who creates as one who creates not? Will you not then remember?" [(16): 17] So Tawheed al-Uluhiyyah is that which the Messengers called to.

There still exists dispute concerning Tawheed al-Uluhiyyah between the people of Tawheed and the people of misguidance. Those who posses the sound Aqeedah call those who have been misguided from Tawheed al-Uluhiyyah and returned to the Deen of the Mushrikeen by worshiping the graves and tombs, venerating saints and approving for them attributes of Lordship - that they should return back to the sound Aqeedah and single out Allah in His worship. They should abandon this dangerous matter which has overtaken them because it is the religion of the Jahiliyyah, rather it is worse than Jahiliyyah because the people of Jahiliyyah would become sincere to Allah at times of hardships and associate partners with Him only during ease.

But the Shirk of these misled people is continuous during ease and hardship. Rather their shirk during hardship is more severe! If matters become worse for them, you hear them calling out to the awliya and the dead for help whereas the Mushrikeen (at the time of Allah's Messenger   ) would sincerely invoke Allah when they were afflicted with calamity...

So, Tawheed al-Uluhiyyah was the call of all the Messengers who called their nations to worship Allah alone and it is this category of Tawheed which was the cause of dispute (between the Prophets and their nations) and it is for this category of Tawheed that the Messengers fought the Mushrikeen until they abandoned shirk and this is the meaning of La ilaha illa Allah because ilah means the deity and therefore we understand La ilaha illa Allah to mean there is no true deity (worthy of being worshiped) except Allah. Ilah does not mean – as some misguided explain – the One who is capable of creating and originating!"

[end quote from Mujmal]

Read more about the deviant interpretations
of La ilaha illa Allah in the Appendix, p. 55

The following (until pg.44) is adapted from the book, Aqeedah at-Tawheed by Shaikh Saleh ibn Fawzan ibn Abdullah al-Fawzan

Meaning of al-Ibadah

The basic meaning of Ibadah is humility and submission. In the Sharee'ah, it has numerous definitions but their meaning is one. From them are:

- To worship Allah in conformity to what He has ordered upon the tongues of His Messenger.

- Utmost submission with utmost love for Allah.

- A more general meaning of al-Ibadah is that it is a comprehensive term for everything that Allah loves and is pleased with from speech and actions - inwardly and outwardly.

Worship is categorized as worship of the heart, tongue and limbs.

- Fear, hope, love, reliance, desire, reverence are worships of the heart.

- Glorifying Allah, thanking Allah by the tongue and heart are worships of the heart and tongue.

- Salaat, Zakaat, Hajj are worships of the limbs and heart.

Apart from these, there are numerous other worships of the heart, tongue and limbs.

Allah created everything for the purpose of worship.

Allah says, "I created not the jinn and humans except that they should worship Me (Alone). I seek not any provision from them nor do I ask that they should feed Me." [Soorah an-Najm (51): 56]

Allah informs us (in this verse) that the wisdom behind creating the Jinn and humans is that they establish His worship. However, Allah is not in need of their worship but they are in need of Him due to their poverty before Him - so they (ought to) worship Him in compliance with His Sharee'ah. So,

- He who does not worship Allah is arrogant.

- He who worships Him and others with Him is a Mushrik (one, who associates partners with Allah).

- He who worships Him by other than what He has legislated is a Mubtadi (an innovator).

- He who worships Him Alone with that which He has legislated is a Mumin (believer) and Muwahhid (one who establishes Tawheed in its correct manner).

Ibadah has many forms. It includes all forms of outward obedience of the tongue and the limbs and inward obedience of the heart like remembrance of Allah, reciting the Qur'aan, Salaat, Zakaat, Siyam, Hajj, commanding the good and forbidding the evil, doing good to the relatives, orphan, poor and travelers.

Similarly, love of Allah and His Messenger, fear of Allah and returning to him, sincerity in the Deen, (Sabr) being patient with His Rule and (Radaa) being pleased with His Decree, (Tawakkul) reliance upon Him, (Rajaa) hope in His Mercy, (Khauf) fear from His punishment (are worships of the heart).

> Ibadah includes all the actions of a Mu'min (believer) if he intends to worship Allah with them or that which aids this purpose. Even his habits (become worship) if he intends to worship Allah with them like sleep, food, drink, buying and selling, seeking provision and marriage. All actions if accompanied by good intentions turn into worship and worship is thus not limited to the known rituals.

Misunderstandings in defining al-Ibadah

Ibadah is Tawqeefiyah meaning nothing can be legislated concerning it except with a proof from the Book and the Sunnah. Any act which is not legislated by Allah is considered a rejected innovation as the Messenger of Allah said, "Whoever performs an action that is not ordered by us is rejected." [Agreed upon] meaning the action is rejected and not accepted. Moreover, it is recorded as a sin because it is disobedience.

The correct Manhaj (manner) of performing the legislated worship is moderation between being easy and harsh and between laziness and extremism. Allah says to His Messenger, "So stand you firm and straight as you are commanded and those (your companions) who turn in repentance (unto Allah) with you, and transgress not (Allah's legal limits)." [Soorah Hud (11): 112]

In this noble verse, the correct Manhaj to perform worship has been mentioned, which is to adhere to moderation without negligence or extremism – and according to the legislation, 'as you are commanded.'

Allah reinforced the above with His Saying, "and transgress not (Allah's legal limits)." Transgression is to go beyond bounds due to harshness and stubbornness and this is exaggeration.

Three Companions of Allah's Messenger considered their deeds insignificant, one of them said, 'I will fast and not break my fast.' And another said, 'I will pray and not sleep.' And the third said, 'I will not marry women.' The Prophet said, 'As for me then I fast and break my fast and I marry women so whoever turns away from my Sunnah is not from me.' [Agreed upon]

Two misguided groups regarding the issue of Ibadah

The first group fell short in their understanding of Ibadah and became lenient in performing it until they cancelled out many forms of worship, and reduced the meaning of worship to certain actions and some rituals that are performed in the mosques. According to them worship does not extend over the house, office, workshop, streets, neither in their dealings, politics, in seeking judgment to their dispute, nor in any other aspect of life.

Yes, the mosque has a virtue, and it is obligatory to perform five daily prayers in it, but worship envelopes all aspects of a Muslim's life - inside the mosque and outside it.

The second group overstressed in implementing worship to the extent of exaggeration; they raised the Mustahabb (recommended) actions to the level of Wajib (obligatory), and prohibited some Mubah (permissible actions), and declared deviant and mistaken those people, who disagreed with their Manhaj (way) and proved their understanding to be incorrect.

And the best guidance is the guidance of Muhammad and the worst of affairs are the newly invented matters.

Pillars of the Correct Worship

Worship centers around three pillars
    (a) love
    (b) fear
    (c) hope

Worship comprises all of these; love with humbleness, and fear with hope. Allah says describing His believing slaves, "whom He will love and they will love Him." [Soorah al-Maida (5):54] and, "those who believe, love Allah more (than anything else)." [Soorah al-Baqarah (2):165] He said describing His Messengers and Prophets, "Verily, they used to hasten on to do good deeds and they used to call on Us with hope and fear and used to humble themselves before Us." [Soorah al-Ambiya (21): 90]

Some of the Salaf have said,

- He who worships Allah with love alone is a Zindeeq (heretic).

- He who worships Allah with hope alone is a Murjee

- He who worships Allah with fear alone is a Hurooree (from the Khawarij)

- He who worships Allah with love, fear and hope is a Mumin Muwahhid (believer).

Shaikhul-Islam Ibn Taymiyyah has mentioned this is his essay, 'al-Ubodiyah,' and he also writes,

> "Thus, the Deen of Allah is worship, obedience and submission to Him. As for Ibadah, its original meaning also denotes lowliness and submission. One says, 'a pathway that is mu'abbad,' i.e. it has become smoothed out because of being treaded upon. However, the Ibadah that has been enjoined (upon us) encompasses the meaning of submission along with the meaning of love. It embodies the utmost degree of submission to Allah through utmost degree of love to Him...
>
> One who submits to a person whilst possessing hatred for him is not an aabid (worshipper) of him and if he was to love someone and at the same time does not submit to him, he is likewise not an aabid of him as is the case of a man who loves his child and friend.
>
> Consequently, only one of the two (qualities) is not sufficient as far as the Ibadah of Allah is concerned. It is necessary that Allah be the most beloved - above all else - to the abd (the slave) and he should hold Allah to be the greatest of all. Indeed none other than Allah deserves total love and submission..." [end quote] [See, Majmoo at-Tawheed an-Najdiyah, p.549]

Allamah Ibnul-Qayyim (rahimahullah) writes in Nuniyyah:

> "Worship of Allah is utmost love for Him,
> along with the worshipper's submission,
> these are the two axis upon which the orbit of Ibadah
> revolves.
>
> It does not revolve until the axis are established, and
> that which causes it to turn is the command of the
> Messenger, not desires, soul or Shaytan."

Allamah Ibnul-Qayyim (rahimahullah) likened the revolution of worship upon love and submission for the beloved (i.e. Allah) - to the revolution of a celestial body upon its axis. He mentioned that the revolution of worship is by the command of the Messenger and what he has ordered - not desire or what the soul or the Shaytan orders him because such would not be worship. So the orders of the Messenger revolves the orbit of worship - not innovations, desires or blind-following of the forefathers."

[end quote from Aqeedah at-Tawheed]

Faith in the Oneness of Allah's Names and Attributes

Those who associate themselves to Islam have split-up with regards to this category of Tawheed. They have split into various groups based on the following three principles;

a) Believing in (all) the Names and Attributes of Allah,
b) Believing in the Names of Allah without believing in His Attributes
c) Believing in the Names of Allah and some Attributes of Allah

There are also those extremists who even deny the Names of Allah and say, "Allah has no Names and no Attributes. We have left them (i.e., the Qur'aanic verses and Ahadeeth which speak about the Names and Attributes of Allah) because they are unclear."

(the first group) As-Salaf as-Saleh (the pious predecessors) affirmed the Names and Attributes of Allah in their obedience to what is mentioned in the Saying of Allah, "(all) the Most Beautiful Names belong to Allah, so call on Him by them," [Soorah al-A'raf (7): 180]

This (above-mentioned verse) is a proof of affirming the Names of Allah and the following verse is a proof of affirming Allah's Attributes, "For Allah is the highest description." [Soorah an-Nahl (16): 60] The meaning of, 'highest description,' is the complete description.

These are two general verses affirming two issues;
(i) The Names of Allah
(ii) The Attributes of Allah

There are numerous details in the Qur'an and the Sunnah (concerning the Names and the Attributes of Allah).

(the second group) Those who affirm Allah's Names without

affirming His Attributes say, "Allah is Samee (All-Hearing) without a Hearing, He is Baseer (All-Seeing) without sight.' This is well-known in the Mu'tazilah Madhhab.

The third group affirms the Names of Allah and some Attributes. They affirm seven attributes and negate all the others, and those seven Attributes are: (i) Life, (ii) Knowledge, (iii) Power, (iv) Hearing, (v) Sight, (vi) Will and (vii) Speech.

> As-Safaraanee gathered them in his saying,
> "He has life, Speech and Sight, Hearing,
> Will, Knowledge and Power..."

Those who affirm the Names and some Attributes of Allah (i.e., the third group) argue, "We affirm these Attributes because (only) these attributes are approved by the intellect while the rest are not approved by the intellect, so we do not affirm them.

(Intellectual proofs of the third group are;)

> The existing creation proves that it was originated. Its origin proves power (to originate) because there cannot be origination without power. This is an intellectual proof (for Allah's Attribute of Power).

> Choice proves Will - i.e. (the choice/will) to make the sun, the moon, the sky and the earth. All this proves the Will of their Creator, Who Willed that these things should be as they are. This is also an intellectual proof (for Allah's Attribute of Will)

> If we look into the creation, we find it to be a perfectly coherent creation. Coherence proves knowledge because an ignorant cannot create coherence.

So, three Attributes have been affirmed for Allah (i) Power, (ii) Will and (iii) Knowledge and these three cannot exist except with life and therefore they affirm that Allah is Living.

A living would be hearing, seeing and speaking which are attributes of perfection or a living would be blind, deaf and dumb which are attributes of deficiency. So, (they say) it is obligatory to affirm the attribute of perfection for the Living.

So, these are their logical proofs based upon which they affirm seven Attributes for Allah.

If one of them is asked to affirm the attribute of Mercy for Allah, he refuses saying, "I do not affirm Mercy for Allah because I explain it as I believe. I say, Mercy is the Will of doing good, or it is doing good itself." and therefore he does not understand Mercy as an Attribute (of Allah).

But we say, This (understanding/explanation) is wrong. (Moreover,) We can rationally prove the Mercy (of Allah) through the effects of Allah's Mercy that we witness (in the world). Blessings (of Allah for His creatures) that cannot be enumerated are due to the Mercy (of Allah). Cruelty from which we are protected is also due to the Mercy (of Allah). These blessings prove the Attribute of Mercy (for Allah).

The proof of blessings for affirming the Mercy of Allah is stronger than the proof of choice for affirming the Will of Allah because the former is known by both the common and the learned. Despite this, they deny the Attribute of Mercy and affirm the Attribute of Will.

From this instance, it becomes known that whosoever forsakes the path of the Salaf, he is in constant decline because there is no harmony in falsehood. "Do they not consider the Qur'an carefully? Had it been from other than Allah, they would surely have found therein much contradiction." [Soorah an-Nisa (4): 82]

<u>Our (Ahlus-Sunnah wal-Jama'ah's) belief concerning the Names and Attributes of Allah is that we affirm all the Names and Attributes of Allah that Allah has affirmed for Himself.</u> We purify this affirmation from the two great prohibitions:

- **Tamtheel** (resembling Allah to His creation)

- **Takyeef** (asking how the Names and Attributes are). These two prohibitions are proven by the text (of the Quran and the Sunnah) and also by the intellect.

Allah says,
"There is nothing like unto Him."
[Soorah ash-Shura (42): 11]

"So put not forward similitude for Allah."
[Soorah an-Nahl (16): 74]

"Do you know of any who is similar to Him?"
[Soorah Maryam (19): 65]

There are many texts in the Quran and the Sunnah concerning the prohibition of resemblance.

Rational Proof

(for the Prohibition of Resembling Allah to His creation)

It can never ever be rational that the Creator resembles the creation whilst there is a huge difference between the two:

- The Creator is the One who brings (the creation) into existence (from nothingness).

- The creation is that which is brought into existence.

- The Existence of the Creator is Eternal and Everlasting.

- The creation is not always present and can be destroyed, rather it will perish. "Whatsoever is on it (the earth) will perish. And the Face of your Lord full of Majesty and Honor will abide forever." [Soorah ar-Rahman (55): 26-27]

Some of the Salaf (pious predecessors) said that if you read the verse,

"Whatsoever is on it (i.e., the earth) will perish."

do not stop at this point; continue to read what is mentioned after it,

"the Face of your Lord full of Majesty and Honor
will abide forever."

(One should continue reading) in order to establish the clear distinction between the Creator and the creation, and to know the Perfection of Allah and deficiency of others bedsides Him.

If someone argues that Allah has affirmed a Face for Himself in the verse, "the Face of your Lord full of Majesty and Honor will abide forever." [Soorah ar-Rahman (55): 27]

> (But) I do not understand the Face except like the face of the creation and therefore affirming the Face of Allah necessitates resembling Allah with the creation. (Such is) because the Quran is in Arabic and (the meaning of face) is what is well-known amongst the people, and the most perfect face is the human face. So, the Face of Allah is like the human face.

So, how do we reply?

Reply: This is an incorrect understanding because the Face is attributed to Allah and that which is attributed befits the One, it is attributed to. So, the Face of Allah befits Him, and the human face befits the human.

(For instance), you have a face and the lion has a face, and the cat has a face. So, if we say, the face of a man, the face of a lion and the face of a cat - does this necessitate resemblance?

No one ever says that his face resembles the face of a cat or a lion. So we know from this instance that the face befits the one it is attributed to.

It is thus proven by textual and rational proofs that affirming the Attributes of Allah does not necessitate any resemblance between the Creator and the creation.

The Prohibition of Takyeef

(describing Allah or asking about His description)

The Attributes of Allah cannot be described - neither by actions nor by words.

Textual Proof

(for the prohibition of Takyeef)

"They will never encompass anything of His Knowledge." [Soorah Ta-Ha (20): 110] "They will never encompass anything of His Knowledge." [Soorah al-Baqarah (2): 255]

"Say (O Muhammad   ), "the things that my Lord has indeed forbidden are... saying things about Allah of which you have no knowledge." [Soorah al-A'raf (7): 33]

"Do not follow that which you have no knowledge of. Verily! The hearing and the sight and the heart of each of those you will be questioned (by Allah)." [Soorah al-Isra (17): 33]

Thus, he who describes Allah has said that which he has no knowledge of (because we are not informed about the description of Allah's Attributes).

Rational Proof

for the Prohibition of Takyeef
(describing Allah or asking for description)

It is not possible for anyone to know the description of something except
- after seeing it
- or seeing its like
- or hearing a true information about it

For example, if I were to see something with my own eyes then I would know its description because I have seen it with my own eyes.

(an example of seeing its like is when) someone comes to me and says, "I have purchased a certain model of car." and he describes the car and its color to me. Although I have not seen the actual car, I know this car because I know and have seen the like of it.

An example of true information is when a man comes to me and says, "I have a camel." and he describes its attributes to me and informs me that it has such-and-such marking. Then I will know what the camel is like from hearing information about it.

If we apply this rational principle to the Attributes of Allah, then it is not possible for us to know the Attributes of Allah through any of these sources, because we have neither witnessed it, seen its like nor are we informed about it.

Therefore, some of the scholars said, "If a jahmi asks you, 'how does Allah descend to the lower heaven?' Then reply saying, "Allah has informed us that He descends but He did not inform us how He descends. So we have to believe in what has reached us, and keep silent about that which we have not been informed about.

An example of this is the saying of Malik (rahimahullah) when he was asked (about the verse), "The Most Beneficent Istawa (rose over) the Throne." [Soorah Ta-Ha (20): 5] How does Allah Istawa (rise over the throne)?

Imam Malik dropped his head due to the enormity of the question and in order to produce an appropriate reply until he was sweating. Then he raised his head and replied with his famous statement which is considered the scale of all the Attributes of Allah,

"الاستواء غير مجهول، والكيف غير معقول،
والإيمان به واجب، والسؤال عنه بدعة"

"Istiwa is not unknown,
its description is beyond our understanding,
belief in it is obligatory,
and questioning about it is an innovation."

So we say to every person who asks about the description of an Attribute of Allah, 'You are an innovator. Your job is to believe in that which has reached you and keep silent about that which you are not informed about.'

Appendix

Appendix adapted from the book,
'Aqeedah at-Tawheed'
by Shaikh Saleh ibn Fawzan ibn Abdullah al-Fawzan

Meaning of the two testimonies

La ilaha illAllah is to believe and affirm that no one deserves worship except Allah, holding on to it and acting in accordance with it. 'La ilah' is negating that anybody has the right to be worshiped except Allah, whoever it might be. 'IllAllah' is affirming the Right of Allah Alone to be worshiped. So, the complete meaning of the statement is 'La Ma'bood BiHaqqin illAllah', 'there is no deity truly worthy of being worshiped except Allah.' The word La (there is none), must accompany BiHaqqin (truly worthy of) and it is not permissible to use the word, 'Mawjood' (existing) because it is against reality. There are many deities worshiped other than Allah and (saying, 'La Ma'bood Mawjood illAllah') implies that worship of all these deities is worship of Allah and this is the most false statement and it is the Madhhab (position) of the people of Wahdat al-Wujood (pantheism), who are the most deviant people on the face of the earth. This statement (i.e. the first testimony) has been explained with numerous deviant interpretations, from them are:

1. La Ma'bood illAllah (there is no deity in existence except Allah). This is the most deviant interpretation because it means that every true and false deity is Allah as has been explained above.

2. La Khaliq illAllah (there is no Creator except Allah). This is only a part of the meaning of the statement, but this is not the intent as it only confirms Tawheed ar-Rububiyah, which is not enough (to enter Islam) and is the Tawheed of the

Mushrikeen (those who affirm Allah's Lordship but worship others besides Him).

3. La Hakimiyah illAllah (there is no judgment except for Allah). This is also only a part of the meaning of the statement and is not the intent because it is not enough. Because if one singles out Allah for judgment only and invokes other than Allah, then he has dedicated a form of worship to other than Allah and thus, he is not a muwahhid (one who declares and establishes Tawheed in its correct manner).

All these interpretations are false and incomplete, and we have mentioned them here because they are found in some contemporary books. The correct meaning of the statement according to the Salaf as mentioned before is to say, 'La Ma'bood BiHaqqin illAllah' (there is no deity truly worthy of being worshiped except Allah).

The Meaning of the testimony, Muhammadar-Rasoolullah. It is to affirm inwardly and outwardly that he ﷺ is a slave of Allah and His Messenger to all people, and to act in accordance to it's requirements which are:

a) Obedience to the Prophet ﷺ in everything that he orders
b) Believing in everything he ﷺ has informed us about
c) Refraining from everything that he ﷺ has prohibited
d) Not to worship Allah except in the way he ﷺ has prescribed.

Pillars of the two testimonies

1. La ilaha illAllah has two pillars:

a) The First Pillar: Negation - 'La ilah' negates all forms of Shirk and its types, and necessitates disbelieving in everything that is worshiped other than Allah.

b) The Second Pillar: Affirmation - 'illAllah' affirms that none deserves worship except Allah and requires acting upon it.

The meaning of these two pillars has been mentioned in many verses, like the Saying of Allah, 'Whoever disbelieves in Taghoot and believes in Allah, then he has grasped the most trustworthy handhold that will never break.' [Soorah al-Baqarah (2): 256]

His Saying, 'Whoever disbelieves in Taghoot' is the meaning of the first pillar, i.e., La ilah.

His Saying, 'believes in Allah' is the meaning of the second pillar, i.e., illAllah.

Similarly, the saying of Ibraheem ﷺ which Allah relates in the Qur'aan, "Verily, I am innocent of what you worship, except Him, Who did create me..." [Soorah az-Zukhruf (43): 26-27]

"I am innocent..." is the meaning of negation in the first pillar,

"except Him, Who did create me" is the meaning of affirmation in the second pillar.

2. The Pillars of Muhammadar-Rasoolullah are

two and they are included in our saying, 'Abduhu wa-Rasooluh' (i.e., he   is Allah's slave and Messenger). They negate any exaggeration and inadequacy in his respect. So, he   is Allah's slave and Messenger, and he is the most perfect creation in these two noble attributes.

The meaning of 'slave' here is the worshiper who is owned (by Allah) meaning he is a man created from what all the other humans are created from. What occurs with other humans also occurs with him, as Allah says, 'Say (O Muhammad): 'I am only a man like you.' [Soorah al-Kahf (18): 110] 'Is not Allah Sufficient for His slave?' [(39): 36]

"All praises and thanks be to Allah, Who has sent down to His slave..." [Soorah al-Kahf (18): 1]

"Glorified be He (Allah), Who took His slave for a journey by night from al-Masjid-al-Haram..." [Soorah al-Israa (17):1]

The meaning of, 'His Messenger' is that he is sent to all people with the call to Allah, giving them glad tidings (of Paradise) and warning them (against Hell-fire).

The testification contains the following two qualities for him. Negation of any exaggeration and inadequacy in his respect because many of those who claim to be from his Ummah have exaggerated in respecting him until they raised him above the status of a worshiper of Allah to the status of being worshiped besides Allah. They sought help from him and invoked him for that which no one but Allah has the Power to provide such as fulfilling needs and relieving troubles. Whilst others neglected his   message or were negligent in obeying him and relied upon opinions and sayings that were contradictory to what he   came with.

Conditions
of the two testimonies

The Conditions of La ilaha illAllah

La ilaha illAllah has seven conditions. The testification does not benefit him, who (merely) utters the testification - unless he fulfils all seven conditions;

1. Knowledge that negates ignorance
2. Certainty that negates doubt
3. Acceptance that negates rejection
4. Submission that negates abandonment
5. Sincerity that negates Shirk
6. Truthfulness that negates falsehood (hypocrisy)
7. Love that negates hatred

The detailed explanation of these seven conditions is as follows:

1. Al-Ilm – Knowledge. Knowledge of the meaning of the

testification and its intent. For example, what the testimony negates and what it affirms - a knowledge that negates ignorance. Allah says, "except those who bear witness to the truth, and they know..." [Soorah az-Zukhruf (43): 86]

'those who bear witness,' means they witness, 'La ilaha illAllah,'

'and they know,' by their hearts what they witnessed by their tongues. So, he who utters it but does not have the knowledge of it, then the testimony will not benefit him, because he did not believe in the intent of testification.

2. Al-Yaqeen - Certainty. One who testifies should be certain about the meaning of the testification because if one doubts then the testimony will not benefit him. Allah says, "Only those are the believers who have believed in Allah and His Messenger, and afterward doubt not..." [Soorah al-Hujurat (49): 15]

So, if he doubts, then he is a hypocrite. Allah's Messenger said, "Whoever you meet behind this wall testifying 'La ilaha illAllah,' with certainty in his heart, then give him the glad tiding of Jannah." [Saheeh al-Bukharee] Thus, he who does not have certainty in his heart does not deserve to enter Jannah.

3. Al-Qubool - Acceptance. Acceptance of what the testimony necessitates like, worshiping Allah alone, and abandoning the worship of other than him. He, who utters the testimony but does not accept it and does not adhere to it, then he is from among those regarding whom Allah says, 'Truly, when it was said to them, 'La ilaha ill-Allah', they puffed themselves up with pride (i.e. denied it). And (they) said, 'Are we going to abandon our aaliha (false gods) for the sake of a mad poet? [Soorah as-Saffat (37): 35-36] This is the situation of the grave-worshipers of today; they say, 'La ilaha illAllah,' but do not refrain from worship of the graves and thus, they are not accepting the meaning of, 'La ilaha illAllah.'

4. Al-Inqiyad - Submission. Submitting to what the testimony indicates. Allah says, "Whosoever submits his face (himself) to Allah, while he is a Muhsin (doer of good) then he has

grasped the most trustworthy handhold..." [Soorah Luqmaan (31):22] The most trustworthy handhold is, 'La ilaha illAllah,' and the meaning of, 'submits his face,' is sincere submission to Allah.

5. As-Sidq – Truthfulness. To witness the testimony

with truthfulness in one's heart. He, who utters the testimony while his heart is not certain about its truthfulness is a lying hypocrite. Allah says, "and of mankind, there are some (hypocrites) who say, 'We believe in Allah and the Last Day' while in fact, they believe not. They (think to) deceive Allah and those who believe, while they only deceive themselves, and perceive (it) not! In their hearts is a disease (of doubt and hypocrisy) and Allah has increased their disease. A painful torment is theirs because they used to lie." [Soorah al-Baqarah (2): 8-10]

6. Ikhlas – Sincerity. It is purification of the action from all

blemishes of Shirk, such that one does not utter it for the pleasures of the world, riyaa (showing off) or fame as is known from the authentic Hadeeth, "Allah has prohibited the Fire for the one, who says, 'La ilaha illAllah' seeking by it, the face of Allah." [Agreed upon]

7. Muhabbah – Love. Love for the testimony, its intent and

those who act upon its prerequisites. Allah says, "And of mankind are some who take (for worship) others besides Allah as rivals (to Allah). They love them as they love Allah. But those who believe love Allah more (than anything else)." [Soorah al-Baqarah (2):165] So, the people of, 'La ilaha illAllah' love Allah with sincere love while the people of Shirk love Him and others besides Him and this negates the prerequisites of La ilaha illAllah.

Conditions
of, 'Muhammadar-Rasoolullah'

1. Affirming his   Prophethood and having faith in it within the heart.

2. Verbally declaring it and affirming it outwardly through the tongue.

3. Following him by acting upon the truth he came with, and refraining from the evil that he has forbidden.

4. Believing in what he has informed about - from the unseen of the past and the future.

5. Loving him more than one's self, wealth, children, parents and the whole of humanity.

6. Giving precedence to his   sayings over everybody, and acting upon his Sunnah.

Prerequisites of the two testimonies

The Prerequisite of 'La ilaha illAllah' is to abandon the worship of all other deities other than Allah, as we say in our testimony, 'La ilaha,' and worshiping Allah alone as we say in our testimony, 'illAllah.' However, many of those who say the testimony contradict its prerequisites, and affirm the Uluhiyah of the creation; the graves, tombs, trees and stones, which is negated by Allah. These people believe that Tawheed is a bidah and reject those who call them to it and criticize those who sincerely worship Allah.

The prerequisite of 'Muhammadar-Rasoolullah' is to follow him, believe in him, refrain from that which he has forbidden, restrict one's actions to his Sunnah and leave that which contradicts it from the newly invented matters, and give precedence to his sayings over everybody else's sayings.

Nullifiers
of the two testimonies

Nullifiers of the two testimonies are the nullifiers of Islam because it is the two testimonies that one pronounces in order to enter Islam. Uttering the two testimonies is affirming their intent, and being steadfast in establishing their prerequisites like fulfilling the rituals of Islam. If one forsakes this steadfastness then he has invalidated the pledge he took when he uttered the two testimonies.

The nullifiers of Islam are many and the scholars have collected them in books of Fiqh under the title, 'The Chapter of Riddah (Apostasy).' However, the most important of them are ten, which have been mentioned by Shaikhul-Islam Muhammad Ibn Abdul Wahhab (rahimahullah) (they are the following).

1. Shirk in the worship of Allah. Allah says, "Verily! Allah forgives not (the sin of) setting up partners in worship with Him, but He forgives whom he pleases - sins other than that..." [Soorah an-Nisa (4): 116] and, "Verily, whosoever sets up partners in worship with Allah, then Allah has forbidden Paradise for him, and the Fire will be his abode. And for the Zalimoon (polytheists and wrongdoers) there are no helpers." [Soorah al-Maida (5): 72] and it includes sacrificing for other than Allah, like tombs and jinn.

2. Setting up intercessors between oneself and Allah, invoking them, asking them for intercession and relying upon them. One who does this is considered by consensus a disbeliever.

3. He who does not declare the Mushrikeen (those who associate partners in worship with Allah) to be disbelievers, or doubts their disbelief, or approves their Madhhab (faith, creed) has disbelieved (in Allah).

4. Believing that the guidance of someone other than the Prophet is more complete than his guidance, or that the ruling of other than him is better, like those who prefer the ruling of the tawagheet (pl. of Taghoot meaning things worshiped other than Allah) over the ruling of Allah's Messenger and they prefer manmade laws to Islam.

5. He, who hates something from that which the Messenger came with, has disbelieved, even if he was acting upon it.

6. He, who mocks at something from the Religion of the Messenger, its rewards or punishments, has disbelieved. The proof of this is the Saying of Allah, "Say, 'Was it at Allah, and His Ayat and His Messenger that you were mocking? Make no excuse, you have disbelieved after you had believed." [Soorah Tawbah (9): 65-66]

7. Magic. From the types of magic is that which causes unity and disunity among people (like causing separation of the husband from his wife or causing him to love her). He, who does this or is pleased with it, has disbelieved. The proof is the Saying of Allah, "...but neither of these two (angels) taught anyone (such things) until they had said, 'We are only for trial, so disbelieve not (by learning this magic from us).'" [Soorah al-Baqarah (2): 102]

8. Aiding and cooperating with the Mushrikeen (disbelievers) against the Muslims. The proof is the Saying of Allah, "If any amongst you takes them as Awliya, then surely he is one of them. Verily, Allah guides not those people who are the Dhalimoon (polytheist and wrongdoers and unjust)." [Soorah al-Maidah (5): 51]

9. He, who believes that some people can be excused from the Sharee'ah of Muhammad , just like Khidr was not liable to the Sharee'ah of Moosa , is a disbeliever.

   I (i.e., Shaikh Saleh al-Fawzan) say, 'this is just like what the extremist Sufis believe that they reach a stage (through their piety), where they are not in need of following the Messenger

10. Turning away from the religion of Allah, neither learning it, nor acting upon it. The proof is the Saying of Allah, 'But those who disbelieve, turn away from that whereof they are warned." [Soorah al-Ahqaf (46): 3] "And who does more wrong than he, who is reminded of the Ayaat (proofs, evidences, verses, lessons, signs, revelations, etc.) of his Lord, then he turns aside therefrom? Verily, We shall exact retribution from the Mujrimoon (criminals, disbelievers, polytheist, sinners, etc.)." [Soorah as-Sajdah (32): 22]

Shaikhul-Islam Muhammad Ibn Abdul Wahhab (rahimahullah) said,

"There is no difference if one does any of them (the above nullifiers) jokingly, seriously or in fear, except under force. They are all very dangerous and most likely to happen. So, it is necessary for a Muslim to be aware of them, and fear them for himself. And we seek Allah's protection from that which brings about His Anger and severe punishment."

Legislation (Tashree')
is the (sole) Right of Allah

The meaning of Tashree' (legislation) is (the guidelines/rules) that Allah has revealed for His slaves, like the way (Manhaj) they should follow in beliefs and actions, Tahleel (making things Halaal) and Tahreem (making things Haraam). Thus, it is not allowed for anyone to proclaim anything Halaal unless Allah declares it Halaal, or proclaim anything Haraam unless Allah declares it Haraam. Allah says, "Say not concerning that which your tongues put forth falsely, 'This is lawful and this is forbidden,' so as to invent lies against Allah." [Soorah an-Nahl (16): 116]

"Say (O Muhammad to these polytheist), 'Tell me, what provision Allah has sent down to you! And you have made of it lawful and unlawful.' Say (O Muhammad), 'Has Allah permitted you (to do so), or do you invent a lie against Allah?'" [Soorah Yunus (10): 59]

Allah has thus forbidden Tahleel and Tahreem without a proof from the Book and the Sunnah. He has informed us that it is a lie against Allah just like He informed us that he, who makes something obligatory or forbidden without a proof has made himself a partner with Allah in something that is special of Him Alone, and it is Tashree' (legislation). Allah says, "Or have they partners with Allah (false gods), who have instituted for them a religion which Allah has not allowed." [Soorah ash-Shuraa (42): 21]

He, who obeys such a Musharri' (one, who makes Tashree') other than Allah and he knows it and is pleased with it, then he has associated a partner with Allah. Allah says, "If you obey them, then you would indeed be Mushrikoon." [Soorah al-An'aam (6): 121]

meaning, he who follows those who make Halaal (permissible) what Allah has made Haraam (prohibited) - he has committed Shirk.

Allah has informed us that those who followed the monks and rabbis in their making Halaal what Allah had made Haraam and their making Haraam what Allah had made Haraam - that they had taken their monks as gods besides Allah. Allah says, "They (Jews and Christians) took their rabbis and their monks to be their lords besides Allah..." [Soorah at-Tawbah (9): 31]

When Adee Ibn Hatim heard this verse, he said, "O Messenger of Allah. We didn't worship them."

The Messenger of Allah said, "Did they not make Haraam what Allah made Halaal and you all made it Haraam, and they made Halaal what Allah made Haraam and you all made it Halaal?"

He replied, "Certainly."

The Prophet of Allah said, "That is your worship to them." [At-Tirmidhee (3/247)]

Shaikh Abdur-Rahman Ibn Hasan said, "In this Hadeeth, is a proof that obedience to monks and rabbis while disobeying Allah is worshiping them. It is Major Shirk which Allah does not forgive, as Allah says at the end of the verse, "while they (Jews and Christians) were commanded to worship none but One Deity. La ilaha illa Huwa (none has the right to be worshiped but He). Praise and glory be to Him, (far above is He) from having the partners they associate (with Him)." [Soorah at-Tawbah (9): 31]

Similar is the Saying of Allah, "Eat not (O believers) of that (meat) on which Allah's Name has not been pronounced (at the time of the slaughtering of the animal), for, surely it is Fisq (a sin and disobedience of Allah). And certainly, the Shayateen (devils) do inspire their friends (from mankind) to dispute with you, and if you obey them [by making al-Maytatah (a dead animal) legal by eating it], then you would indeed be Mushrikoon (polytheist) [because they (devils and their friends) made lawful to you to eat that which Allah has made unlawful to eat and you obeyed them by considering it lawful to eat, and by doing so you worshiped them, and to worship others besides Allah is polytheism]." [Soorah al-An'aam (6): 121]

Many people fall into this with regards to those whom they make Taqleed of (i.e., blind-following) due to their lack of concern for a proof (from the Book and the Sunnah) when the person they make Taqleed of differs (with the Qur'aan and the Sunnah). Such an act is from this form of Shirk (i.e., Shirk in Tashree')." [end quote]

So, adherence to the Legislation of Allah and abandoning the Legislation of other than Him is from the prerequisites of La ilaha illAllah. And Allah is the Source of help.

Manhaj (way)
of the Ahlus-Sunnah wal-Jama'ah concerning the Names and Attributes of Allah

The Manhaj (way) of the Ahlus-Sunnah wal-Jama'ah from the Salafus-Salih and those who followed them is to affirm the Names and Attributes of Allah as they have been mentioned in the Book and the Sunnah, and their Manhaj is built on the following principles:

1. They approve the Names and Attributes of Allah as it has been mentioned in the Book and the Sunnah with their apparent meaning indicated by the words and they do not interpret it contrary to its apparent meaning nor change its words or what they indicate.

2. They negate any resemblance between the Attributes of Allah and the creation, Allah says, "There is nothing like unto Him, and He is the All-Hearer, the All-Seer." [Soorah ash-Shuraa (42): 11]

3. They do not exceed what has been mentioned in the Qur'aan and the Sunnah in affirming the Names and Attributes of Allah. What Allah and His Messenger have affirmed, they affirm it and what Allah and His Messenger have denied, they deny it and matters in which Allah and His Messenger are silent, they are silent.

4. They believe that the texts mentioning the Names and Attributes of Allah are Muhkam (clear), whose meaning and

explanation is understood, and they are not Mutashabih (unclear). They do not hold back its meaning, as they have been accused of, by those who lie against them, or those who do not know their Manhaj from among contemporary writers.

5. They do not speak about how the Attributes of Allah are and do not even research them.

Refuting those, who deny all the Attributes of Allah or deny some of them

Those who deny the Names and Attributes of Allah are of three categories:

1. Jahmiyah: They are the followers of Jahm Ibn Safwan and they deny all the Names and Attributes of Allah.

2. Mutazilah: They are the followers of Wasil Ibn Ataa, who deserted the circles of Hasan Basree. They affirm the Names of Allah as if they were just words without meaning, and they deny all the Attributes of Allah.

3. Ashaairah and Maturidiyah and those who follow them. They affirm the Names of Allah and some Attributes and deny some. The notion/pretext upon which they have built their Madhhab is, 'to refrain from any resemblance of Allah to His Creation.' They claim that sharing of the name, attribute and the meaning (between the creation and Allah) necessitates likeness in reality and this means resembling Allah with His Creation in their view. So, they have imposed the following two matters upon themselves:

a) Making Taweel (false interpretation) of the texts of the Names and Attributes of Allah from their apparent meaning, like interpreting the Face to mean His Essence, and His Hands to mean His Generosity.

b) Making Tafweed (leave the meaning to Allah) of the Names and Attributes of Allah to Him. So, they say, 'Allah alone Knows what it means,' along with their belief that they are not to be accepted upon their apparent meaning.

The first group known to have denied the Names and Attributes of Allah were some Arab pagans about whom Allah revealed, "Thus have We sent you (O Muhammad) to a community before whom other communities have passed away, in order that you might recite unto them what We have inspired you, while they disbelieve in the Most Beneficent (Allah)." [Soorah ar-Ra'd (13): 30]

The reason behind the revelation of this verse is that when the Quraysh heard the Messenger of Allah   mention (Allah with the Name) Rahman (the Most Beneficent), they denied it. So, Allah revealed, "...while they disbelieve in the Most Beneficent (Allah)."

Ibn Jareer mentioned that it was during the treaty of Hudaibiyah, when the writer began to put into writing the treaty between the Quraysh and the Messenger of Allah, he started with, 'Bismillah ar-Rahman ar-Raheem' (In the Name of Allah, the Most Beneficent, the Most Merciful). The Quraysh objected to it saying, 'We do not know who Rahmaan is.'

Ibn Jareer also reported from Ibn Abbas, 'The Messenger of Allah used to invoke (Allah) with the words, 'O Rahman, O Raheem.' The

Mushrikeen said, 'He claims to call upon one, but he invokes two.' So, Allah revealed, "Say (O Muhammad), 'Invoke Allah or invoke the Most Beneficent (Rahmaan), by whatever name you invoke Him (it is the same), for to Him belong the Best Names." [Soorah al-Isra (17): 110]

And Allah said in Soorah Furqan, "When it is said to them, 'Prostrate to the Most Beneficent (Allah)! They say, 'And what is the Most Beneficent?" [Soorah al-Furqan (25): 60]

So, these Mushrikeen are the predecessors of the Jahmiyah, Mu'tazilah and Asha'irah, and all those who deny about Allah what He has affirmed for Himself, or His Messenger has affirmed for Him from the Names and Attributes of Allah. What evil predecessors for evil successors…!

A Rebuttal

They can be rebutted is many different ways:

1. First Approach. Allah, the Exalted, affirmed for Himself Names and Attributes, and His Messenger   too affirmed for Him. Denying them for Allah or denying some of them is denying what Allah and His Messenger   have affirmed. This implies contradicting Allah and His Messenger.

2. Second Approach. The existence of some attributes in the creation and some names being used by them does not imply resemblance between Allah and the creation. Because the Names and Attributes of Allah are special to Him, and the Names and Attributes of the creation are particular to them. Just like Allah has an existence, which does not resemble the existence of the creation, similarly He has Names and Attributes that do not resemble the Names and Attributes of the creation. Likeness in the Name and the general meaning does not necessitate likeness in reality. Allah has called Himself Aleem (All-Knowing), Haleem (All-Wise), and He also called some of His slaves Aleem, He said, "they gave him glad tidings of (Aleem) an intelligent son, having knowledge (about Allah and His religion of True Monotheism)." [Soorah adh-Dhariyat (51): 28] meaning Ishaaq. And He named the other Haleem, "So We gave him the glad tidings of (Haleem) a forbearing boy." [Soorah as-Saffat (37): 101] meaning Isma'eel. So, One Aleem is not like the other, similarly, One Haleem is not like the other.

And He called Himself, "Truly, Allah is Ever All-Hearer (as-Samee), All-Seer (al-Baseer)." Similarly, He has named some of His slaves Samee and Baseer. He said, "Verily, We have created man from Nutfah drops of mixed semen (of man and woman), in order to try him, so We made him hearer, seer." [Soorah al-Insan (76): 2] So, One Samee is not like the other and One Baseer is not like the other.

And He called Himself ar-Raouf (full of kindness) and ar-Raheem (Most Merciful), "Verily, Allah is, for mankind, full of Kindness, Most Merciful." [Soorah al-Hajj (22): 65] and He called some of His slaves, Rouf and Raheem, He said, "Verily, there has come unto you a Messenger (Muhammad) from amongst yourselves (i.e. whom you know well). It grieves him that you should receive any injury or difficulty. He (Muhammad) is anxious over you (to be rightly guided, to repent to Allah, and beg Him to pardon and forgive your sins, in order that you may enter Paradise and be saved from the punishment of the Hellfire), for the believers (he is) full of pity, kindness, and mercy.." [Soorah at-Tawbah (9): 128]

Similarly, He described Himself with Attributes, and described His slaves like that, like His Saying, "they will never compass anything of His Knowledge." [Soorah al-Baqarah (2): 255] Thus, He described Himself with Knowledge, and described His slaves with knowledge, "And of knowledge, you (mankind) have been given only a little." [Soorah al-Isra (17): 85] and He said, "We raise to degrees whom We please, but over all those endowed with knowledge is the All-Knowing (Allah)." [Soorah Yusuf (12): 76] and He said, "those who had been given (religious) knowledge said..." [Soorah al-Qasas (28): 80]

He described Himself with strength, "Truly, Allah is All-Strong, All-Mighty." [Soorah al-Hajj (22): 40] and, "Verily, Allah is the All-Provider, Owner of Power, the Most Strong." [Soorah adh-Dhariyat (51): 58] and He described His slaves with power and said, "Allah is He, Who created you in (a state of) weakness, then gave you strength after weakness, then after strength gave (you) weakness and grey hair. He creates what He wills. And it is He, Who is the All-Knowing, the All-Powerful (i.e. Able to do all things)." [Soorah ar-Rum (30): 54] and others.

It is thus known that the Names of Allah are specific to Him and befit Him, and the Names of the creation are specific to them and befit them, and similarity in name and meaning does not necessitate likeness in reality.

And this is apparent, al-Hamdulillah.

3. Third Approach. One, who does not possess perfect

Attributes, does not deserve to be ilah (deity) and this is why Ibraheem   said, "Why do you worship that which hears not, nor sees..." [Soorah Maryam (19): 42] and Allah said in the refutation of those who worshiped the calf, "Did they not see that it could neither speak to them nor guide them to the way?" [Soorah al-A'raaf (7): 148]

4. Fourth Approach. Verily, affirmation of Attributes is perfection, and denying them is deficiency. So, he who does not possess Attributes is either nonexistent or imperfect, and Allah is free from it.

5. Fifth Approach. Making Taweel (changing the meaning) of the Attributes from its apparent meaning has no proof, so it is false. And making Tafweed (leaving the meaning to Allah) means that Allah has addressed us in the Qur'aan with something which we do not understand and He has asked us to ponder over the whole Qur'aan but how can we ponder over it when we do not understand its meaning?

Thus, it has been proved from the above that it is crucial to affirm the Names and Attributes of Allah as they are and deny any resemblance to the creation, as Allah said, "There is nothing like unto Him, and He is the All-Hearer, the All-Seer." [Soorah ash-Shura (42): 11]

So, He negated for Himself resemblance to anything, and affirmed for Himself Hearing and Sight. Therefore, it has been proved that affirming the Attributes (of Allah) does not necessitate resemblance, and it also proves affirming the Attributes along with negation of resemblance. This is the meaning of the saying of Ahlus-Sunnah wal-Jamaa'ah regarding denial and affirmation of the Names and Attributes - 'Affirmation without resemblance and Purification (of Allah from any defect) without denial.'